# STANDING SMALL

## A CELEBRATION OF 30 YEARS OF THE LEGO® MINIFIGURE

# STANDING SMALL

## A CELEBRATION OF 30 YEARS OF THE LEGO® MINIFIGURE

Nevin Martell

# CONTENTS

# INTRODUCTION

You don't have to be tall to make history. Gandhi was 5'3",
Beethoven was 5'3¾", and Picasso was 5'4". Between them they
led India to independence, wrote the Fifth Symphony, and co-
founded the Cubist movement. Well, the LEGO® minifigure has
them all beat. At only 1½ inches tall, it is the shortest superstar of
all time. For over 30 years, the minifigure has made it possible for
children to populate their LEGO worlds with a diverse cast of
characters, from pirates and soldiers to deep-sea divers and aliens.
The minifigure has also become an icon that defies cultural
boundaries and generational divides, consistently standing small
as one of the most revolutionary and popular toys of all time.

The first minifigures in 1978 were based on archetypal characters
such as spacemen, policemen, nurses, and knights and were
facially identical—yellow skin, two black dots for eyes, and a wide
smile—in order to represent people from anywhere in the world.
But a lot has changed in 30 years. In 2003, minifigures were given
realistic skin tones, facial expressions, and molded hair when they
represented real people or named characters from movies or TV
series—starting with LEGO Basketball minifigures and continuing
with the licensed series.

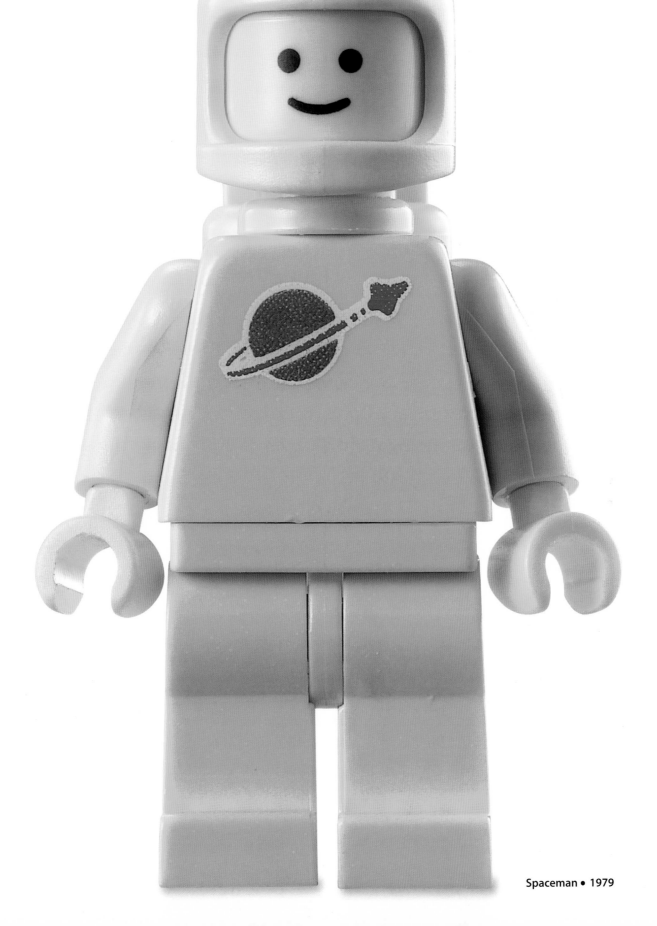

Spaceman • 1979

LEGO® Minifigures have gone global and their ranks have grown to include over 2,500 different characters from around the world—and beyond! Now there are minifigures for movie characters like Harry Potter™, Luke Skywalker™, and *Indiana Jones™*, as well as original LEGO creations like Johnny Thunder, Captain Brickbeard, and the LEGO® EXO-FORCE™ character Hikaru.

Minifigures have digital lives now as well: Computer-animated versions with greater articulation and mobility than real minifigures appear in short films such as the *Star Wars™*-inspired *Revenge of The Brick* and as playable characters in videogames including LEGO® *Star Wars™*: The Video Game, LEGO® *Indiana Jones™*: The Original Adventures, and LEGO® Batman™: The Video Game.

Not only are minifigures perhaps the most diverse toys in the world, they're also the fastest growing. Every second, 3.9 minifigures are sold, which means over 122 million are sold every year, with over 4 billion in existence. At 12 times the population of the United States and 66 times the population of the UK, minifigures represent the biggest population in the world. There are so many of them in the world that they would fill 170 swimming pools.

*Standing Small* is an affectionate look back over the past three decades of the mini icon's reign over the pop culture landscape. The minifigure has changed the lives of millions of people by being the spark that fires their imaginations and their companion on countless adventures. Let's go exploring!

Indiana Jones™ • 2008

# THE ORIGINS OF THE MINIFIGURE

In the mid-1970s LEGO® system designer Jens Nygaard Knudsen and a team of colleagues conceived the first version of the minifigure. He sawed and filed down existing bricks to create a prototype minifigure made of a single inflexible piece with no hands or facial expressions. Knudsen went back to the drawing board and came up with 50 different new prototypes. He began by carving bricks again, but later abandoned this approach and cast his more refined concepts in tin. These new versions were leaps and bounds beyond his originals—they had eyes and a smile, hands that could grip accessories, and their legs and arms could move. The minifigure made its debut in 1978 in LEGO set 600, which featured a policeman and his patrol car. An icon was born and role play was added to the LEGO play experience.

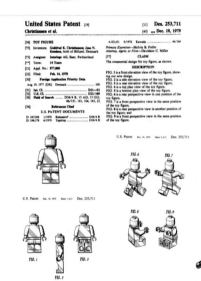

**Minifigure US Patent • 1979**

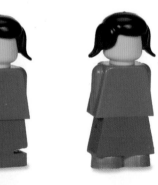

● LEGO Family building figures was launched as art. no. 200 and quickly became the biggest selling product at the time.

● These prototype "red woman" minifigures demonstrate the first use of the hair accessory and the slightly angled torso, which allowed designers to create arms that could swing up and down.

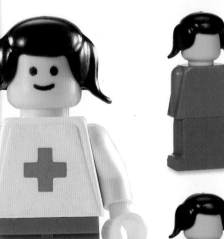

**Doctor • 1978**

Launched in 1975 this was the forerunner of the minifigure

● These "blue man" prototypes feature hinged arms, torsos and legs, which gave the minifigure articulated movement. These first versions of hands were full rings, which designers eventually opened up, so more accessories could be held.

Hinged legs

Hinged arms

Prototype feet

Prototype torso decoration

Prototype head

Policeman • 1978

11

# THE MINIFIGURE

Minifigures are made out of acrylonitrile butadiene styrene, or ABS, a tough plastic compound that makes LEGO® minifigures durable. This plastic is melted into specially designed molds that produce the different parts of the minifigure—head, torso, arms, hands, legs, hips, and the accessories like swords, shovels, and walkie-talkies. Heads and torsos always require further decoration and sometimes the arms and the legs do as well. This meticulous printing process is why the minifigure is the most expensive part of any set. After the paint jobs, arms are attached to the torsos and hands are put into the arms, while legs are snapped onto the hip piece. Finally, all these pieces are bagged, ready for the LEGO builder to put together. Originally, LEGO minifigures came assembled, but now the parts are kept separate so that children get the joy of building their minifigures.

**DID YOU KNOW?**
Each minifigure is exactly four bricks high without a hat.

1 Minifigures on the production line at the Kornmarken factory in Billund, Denmark.

2 Minifigures going through a painting machine having facial features added to their heads. This is also where decoration is added to the minifigures' torsos.

● Each minifigure comes in three parts in LEGO sets; head, torso (which includes arms and hands), hips and legs.

## The Mini Minifigure

● In 2002, the Yoda minifigure became the first to be a different height when shorter legs were introduced. Since then, there have been a number of mini minifigures, including the goblins from the Harry Potter sets and Short Round from the Indiana Jones sets.

Yoda™ • 2002

### DID YOU KNOW?

There are over eight quadrillion possible minifigures to be made from all the parts that have been produced in the last 30 years.

14 karat gold

### DID YOU KNOW?

The most expensive LEGO minifigure is the 14k gold *Star Wars*™ 30th Anniversary C-3PO, which is said to be worth at least $200. Only two were made. There were also Sterling Silver and Bronze versions.

Golden C-3PO • 2007

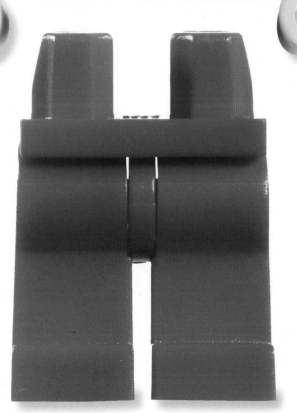

1978 saw the arrival of the first LEGO® minifigures for the new LEGO Town, LEGO Castle, and LEGO Space themes. These three themes are still popular today, along with LEGO Pirates, LEGO Trains, LEGO Vikings, LEGO Wild West, and many more....

POLICE

WANTED

POLICE

POLICE

Police Station • 2008

# LEGO® TOWN

The first minifigure—a police officer—was a part of the LEGO® Town theme in early 1978. Two months later, the first female minifigure arrived in the form of a nurse. Since then, minifigures in this theme have included everything from doctors and racecar drivers to construction workers and chefs.

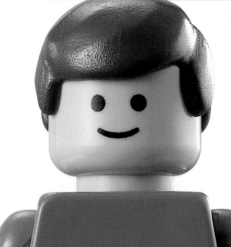

Adult hair first appeared on toddler minifigures that came with Family Figure sets in 1978 ⋯⋯⋯

**Townsperson • 1980**

**Townsperson • 1980**

Ponytail-style hair ⋯⋯⋯

**Townsperson 1985**

Stripes come in red and white (as here) and blue and white

## Typical Townie

● Townspeople are often issued in sets, all with accessories, and all with jobs to do! Many, such as doctors, nurses, and firefighters, wear clothing appropriate to their jobs, but others wear combinations of regular clothes, which includes stripy tops, spotty tops, and many plain colored tops.

**Townsperson • 1992**

**Townsperson • 1982**

**Townsperson • 1984**

**Townsperson • 1985**

**Townsperson • 1989**

## Top Chefs

● The town theme has a lot of cooks in its kitchen. It started out with a single male gourmand, but now there are several additions, including a female chef and a mustached master of the culinary arts.

**Ice Cream Man • 1985**

**Male Chef • 1990**

**Female Chef • 1998**

**Male Chef • 2003**

# Short Arm of the Law

● Criminals can't escape these dedicated lawmen. They are experts at taking down baddies in helicopters or on motorcycles. These cops are in the business of putting bad guys behind bars.

**Some versions of police cap have the word POLICE on front**

**Blue sunglasses for surveillance work**

**This sheriff laid down the law to unruly sports fans!**

**Sheriff's badge**

**Sheriff • 1996**

**Sheriff • 1983**

**Sheriff • 1998**

Townsperson • 1978

**1992 version has a mustache**

Waiter • 1990

**Also comes with life jacket**

Glade Runner Pilot • 1993

**Helmet with visor**

**DID YOU KNOW?**

All the first minifigures had neutral, happy expressions. It was only in 1989 that LEGO® minifigures began to change their facial expressions.

Race Car Driver • 1993

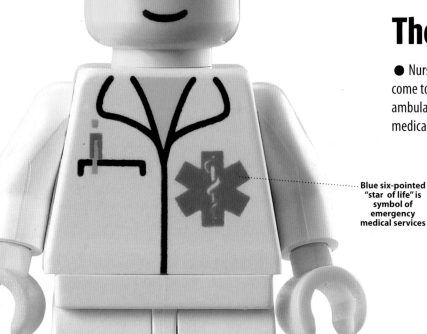

**Blue six-pointed "star of life" is symbol of emergency medical services**

# The Doctors are in

● Nurses and doctors were some of the first minifigures to ever come to the LEGO universe. As hospitals, ambulances, and air-ambulance helicopters were added to the town theme, more medical minifigures were created to help out.

Female Doctor • 1978

Male Doctor • 1981

Female Doctor • 1996

Male Doctor • 1988

Male Doctor • 1996

Male EMT Doctor • 1999

Stunt Pilot • 1993

Stunt Pilot • 1996

Microlight Pilot • 1997

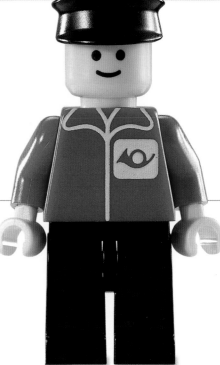

Mailman • 1982

## Going Postal

● In the world of LEGO Town, mailmen are distinguished by a symbol of a French horn on a white background. These red and black minifigures delivered their first letters to townspeople back in 1982.

This cameraman works at the top of a TV tower at a soccer stadium (set 3311)

Sweater with logo of TV company

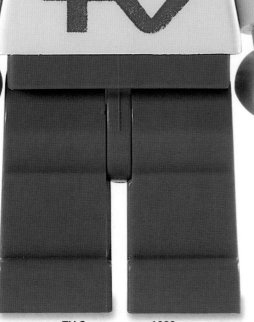

TV Cameraman • 1998

Hard hat

Construction Worker • 1979

Airport Worker • 1988

Life jacket

Coast Guard Pilot • 1996

Trucker • 1993

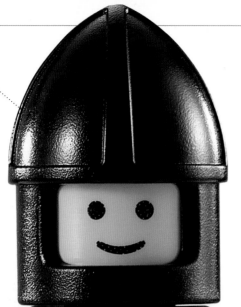

Black Falcons typically wear black helmets with chinstraps

# LEGO® CASTLE

Even though castles have been around since the ninth century, LEGO® Castle didn't debut until 1978. It was one of the first themes introduced—along with LEGO Town and LEGO Space. The first minifigures in the LEGO Castle line were knights, followed by wizards, ghosts, and skeletons! They've jousted, fought dragons, and cast spells, evolving from a historical theme to a medieval fantasy.

Black Falcon crest is a black/white falcon on an inverted background

Black Falcon 1 • 1987

Black Falcon 2 • 1987

## Bad Boys

● The Black Falcons sub-theme was introduced in 1984 when they defeated the Knights after several brutal battles. These sinister soldiers roamed the LEGO universe until 1992, though in 2002, they were brought back for a special reissue of the Black Falcon's Fortress set.

## Fierce Fighters

● The Crusaders are the archenemies of the Black Falcons, constantly getting into skirmishes with them over their territories. The Crusaders' traditional coat-of-arms is an upright crowned lion, though some Crusaders wear a crest of crossed halberts on their chests or shields.

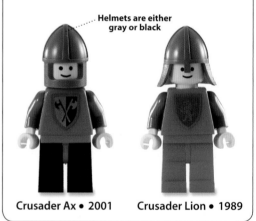

Helmets are either gray or black

Crusader Ax • 2001          Crusader Lion • 1989

## Woodland Warriors

● Loosely based on Robin Hood and his merry men, the Forestmen joined the Castle theme in 1987. When not building tree fortresses, they harass Black Falcon forces.

Feathers are red, black, yellow, blue, or white

Forestman 1 • 1990          Forestman 2 • 1990

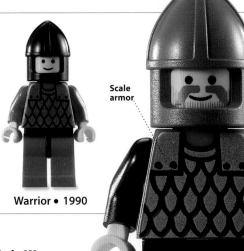

Warrior • 1990

Scale armor

## Beastly Baddies

● The Wolfpack were an evil offshoot of the Forestmen. These lawless looters loved nothing more than to rob luckless travelers journeying through the woods.

Leather armor

Wolfman 1 • 1992

Wolfman 2 • 1992

## This is War

● The first knights in the LEGO Castle theme lived in harmony, but when the Crusaders and the Black Falcons were introduced in 1984, the medieval minifigures went to war.

Warrior • 1993

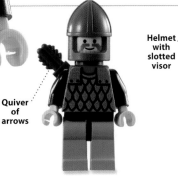

Quiver of arrows

Archer • 1993

Helmet with slotted visor

Warrior • 1995

## DID YOU KNOW?

The largest LEGO castle was built live on Swedish television in 1992 and used over 400,000 bricks!

## DID YOU KNOW?

The first LEGO castles were made out of yellow bricks. The grey bricks weren't introduced until 1984.

Pikesman's helmet

Scale armor doublet

Knight • 2000

Horned helmet

Cedric the Bull • 2000

## LEGO® KNIGHTS' KINGDOM™

● In 2000, a new head-to-head battle for supremacy came to the LEGO Castle theme when King Leo took on the barbarian invaders, who were led by the fearsome Cedric the Bull.

Golden helmet

King Leo • 2000

King Jayko • 2005

Rascus • 2005

Danju • 2005

Santis • 2005

## Hero Knights

● This formidable foursome defends the Kingdom of Morcia from Lord Vladek and the Rogue Knights. Led by the brave King Jayko, they each bring a special skill to the battlefield—speed, agility, strength, and wisdom.

## Dark Lord

● Once an advisor to Morcia's old ruler, King Mathias, Lord Vladek betrayed his liege and attempted to take over the kingdom. When he failed, he took over the neighboring lost kingdom of Ankoria where he plots his revenge.

"Vladmask" is source of Vladek's power

Sorcerer's sword

Vladek wore a red suit of armor before switching to black armor

Scorpion crest

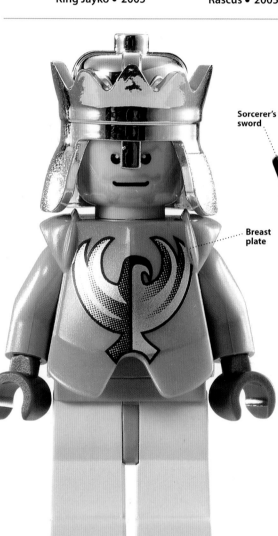

Breast plate

Shadow Knight Vladek • 2006

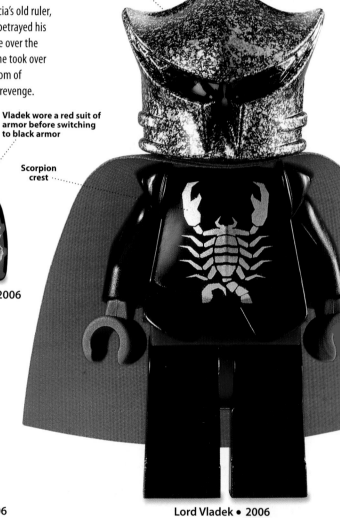

King Jayko • 2006

Shadow Knight • 2006

Lord Vladek • 2006

---

### DID YOU KNOW?

Crossbows, swords, and lances made their first appearance in the Castle theme.

Ax

Shield

Crown Knight • 2007

Crown Princess • 2007

Jester • 2007

Troll Warrior Orc • 2007

## Boo!

● The Ghost first materialized in the Castle theme in 1992. Its introduction marked the move from strictly medieval minifigures to more fantasy-inspired characters. These frightening phantoms prefer to haunt castles, but they've been known to jump out at unsuspecting knights passing the guardshack.

**Ghost • 1997**

### DID YOU KNOW?

The ghost was the first ever specialized minifigure. It features a slip on "sleeve" that glows in the dark.

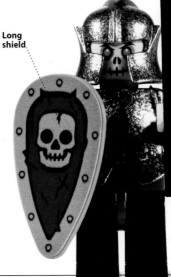

**Evil Wizard • 2007**

## Spell-casters

● The Evil Wizard commands his boney warriors from his dark fortress, Skeleton Tower. This skull-shaped stronghold is protected by a fire-breathing dragon and his counterpart is the Good Wizard.

**Good Wizard • 2007**

Golden broad sword

### DID YOU KNOW?

The wizard's wand was the first glow-in-the-dark accessory.

Double-headed ax

Long shield

Flail

**Crown King • 2007**

**Skeleton Warrior • 2008**

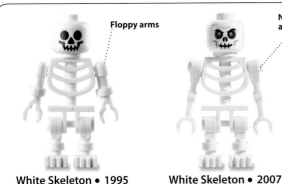

Floppy arms

New poseable arms can hold weapons

**White Skeleton • 1995**

**White Skeleton • 2007**

**Black Skeleton • 2007**

## Skull and Bones

● These frightening fighters are under the spellbinding sway of the Evil Wizard. They are especially terrifying opponents because they can't feel pain and never get tired.

Round shield

**Skeleton Warrior • 2008**

# LEGO® CITY

The LEGO® City theme encompasses a variety of different sub-themes including Police, Construction, Transport, Farm, Fire and Coast Guard. For more than 30 years, sailors, truck drivers, and cops have worked side by side, helping LEGO City remain one of the most successful themes.

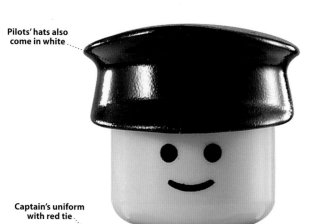

Pilots' hats also come in white

Captain's uniform with red tie

Pilot • 2004

Suitcases can be loaded onto the baggage cart

Airport Worker • 2006

Signal lights

Airport Worker 2 • 2006

## Fly Boys

● A top-notch team of pilots, flight crew, and baggage carriers make sure all passengers get to their final destinations on time and with all their luggage. Along the way, the staff provide ticket holders with a hot meal and a cold drink.

Cargo Plane Captain • 2008

### DID YOU KNOW?

LEGO Town sets were released under the name LEGO City from 2005.

Passenger 1 • 2006

Passenger 2 • 2007

Food service cart

Airport Worker 3 • 2007

Airport Worker 4 • 2007

## Around Town

● It's all about the hustle and bustle in the LEGO City theme. The workers deliver mail, pick up trash, and repair forklifts down at the harbor. These hardworking minifigures always put in a full day's work.

**Mailman comes with letters that be collected from mail box**

Mailman • 2008

Boat Captain • 2007

Harbor Worker • 2007

Heavy Hauler Driver • 2007

Harbor Worker • 2007

**Trash can**

Sanitary Worker • 2007

Construction Worker 1 • 2005

**Gas tank**

Construction Worker 2 • 2007

Construction Worker 3 • 2006

## Men at Work

● These are the guys that built LEGO City from the ground up one brick at a time. In recent years, these workmen have erected towering skyscrapers, hauled big loads in their dump trucks, and plowed huge piles of debris with their bulldozers.

Construction Worker 4 • 2007

Construction Worker 5 • 2005

**Jackhammer**

Construction Worker 7 • 2005

Construction Worker 6 • 2009

**DID YOU KNOW?**
LEGO City minifigures mark the approach of Christmas in LEGO Advent Calendars.

25

Policeman 1 • 2006

Policeman 1 • 2005

EMT Doctor • 2006

Red and white gauge tile forms part of medical equipment

Air Ambulance Doctor • 2006

Camera

Policeman 1 • 2008

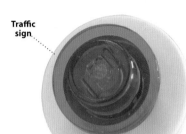
Traffic sign

## Law and Order

● The policeman was the very first LEGO minifigure introduced back in 1978. He came with only a small squad car to help him catch crooks, but now LEGO cops are armed with cutting edge technologies to fight crime.

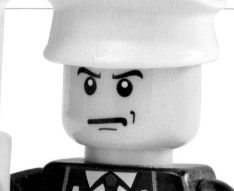
Policeman 2 • 2008

Prisoner 1 and Policeman 3 • 2008

Handcuffs

Prisoner 2 • 2008

Policeman 4 • 2008

Megaphone

Policeman • 2007

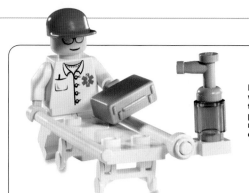

Policeman 5 • 2008

Policeman 2 • 2005

Policeman 6 • 2008

Policeman 2 • 2006

Policeman 3 • 2005

### Star of Life

● These EMT doctors are always on call, ready to respond to any emergency that comes their way. Whether they're stitching up cuts or bandaging bruises, they're prepared for anything.

**Air Ambulance Doctor • 2006**

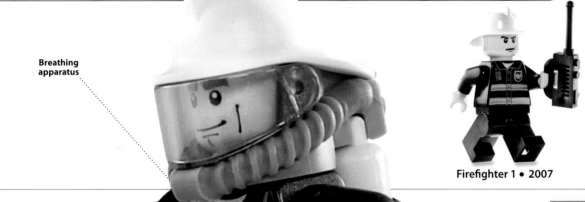

**Doctor • 2006**

**Patient • 2006**

**DID YOU KNOW?**

The word LEGO comes from the Danish phrase LEg GOdt, which means "play well."

Breathing apparatus

**Firefighter 1 • 2007**    **Firefighter 2 • 2005**

**DID YOU KNOW?**

The first Firefighters appeared in 1978 with the introduction of the Fire Station (set 374).

### Hook and Ladder Crew

● When the call comes in, this team of dedicated firefighters are ready to battle big blazes and furious flames to help save their fellow citizens. With the help of trucks, helicopters, boats, and rescue vans, there's no part of the LEGO City they can't reach in their never-ending fight against fire.

**Firefighter 1 • 2005**

Fire extinguisher

**Firefighter 2 • 2007**

**Fire Helicopter Pilot • 2005**

**Firefighter 3 • 2005**

**Firefighter 4 • 2005**

**Firefighter 3 • 2007**

**Firefighter 4 • 2007**

## Urban Legends

● LEGO® City dwellers take all forms in this exciting theme. Whether they're enjoying a cup of morning joe or taking a train into the countryside, these smiling minifigures love their urban lifestyle.

Delivery Man • 2007

Train Passenger • 2007

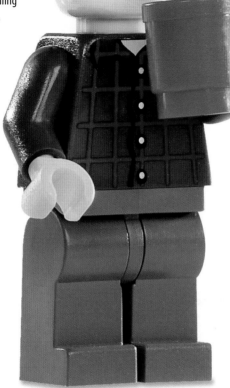

Truck Driver • 2008

Female Worker 1 • 2007

Male Worker • 2007

## Street Scene

● On the bustling streets, busy minifigures like to grab a drink at Café Corner, do their shopping on Market Street, and grab vegetables down at the Greengrocer. The buildings in these sets feature challenging building techniques for advanced LEGO builders.

Female Worker 2 • 2007

Shell helmet

Helicopter Pilot, Patroller, and Rescued Sailor • 2008

Aqualung

Flippers

Diver • 2008

# Always Ready

● Though the Coast Guard sub-theme has been unofficially around since the late-1980s, it didn't become completely recognized until 2008 when a slew of Coast Guard sets centered around helicopters, jet scooters, and speedboats was introduced.

Lifejacket

Patroller • 2008

Patroller • 2008

Helicopter Rescue Swimmer • 2008

# LEGO® WILD WEST

The Sheriff is busy chasing desperate bandits, while the US Cavalry is skirmishing with Native Americans. Sometimes billed as the Western theme, these minifigures first showed up in 1996.

Cowboy 1997

### Bronco Busters
● These rugged frontiersmen can be found testing their luck at Showdown Canyon, causing trouble at Fort Legoredo and dodging bullets at Gold City Junction shoot-outs.

Cowboy • 1996

Large moustache under mask

Bandit • 1996

Bandit • 1997

### DID YOU KNOW?
Revolvers and rifles made their first appearance in the hands of LEGO® Wild West minifigures.

Sheriff badge

Sheriff • 1996

Banker • 1996

Cavalry Colonel • 1996

Cavalry Lieutenant • 1996

Indian Chief • 1997

Buffalo headdress

Medicine Man • 1997

Quiver • 1997

29

# LEGO® TRAINS

All aboard! The Train theme has been around since 1966, though minifigures weren't introduced until 1978. In the more than 40 years of the themes existence, children have been able to build everything from engines and cabooses to Octan rail tankers and the Hogwarts Express™.

Guard • 1982

Railway Employee • 1998

Railway Employee • 1992

## All Aboard

● Engineer Max climbed aboard the LEGO® Express in 2002. Over the years, he has been in charge of the Burlington Northern Santa Fe Locomotive, the Holiday Train, and the Cargo Train.

Railway Engineer • 2009

Railway Employee 1 • 2006

Railway Employee 2 • 2006

Handcart

Luggage

Engineer Max • 2002

Railway Employee 3 • 2003

Conductor Charlie • 2002

Conductor Charlie • 2007

## Tickets, Please!

● Conductor Charlie is a jack of all trades on the train. He collects tickets, helps passengers stow their luggage, and announces the next station stops. During his few spare moments, you can find him relaxing in the caboose.

Conductor Charlie • 2007

## Dining Car Star

● When you get hungry on the train, there's five-star food just a few cars down. The female chef has been feeding passengers since 1998, when she became the first minifigure to sport eyelashes.

Female Chef • 1999

Passenger Train Engineer • 2006

Briefcase

Passenger • 2007

Passenger • 2006

Passenger • 2006

Ticket

Passenger • 2006

Passenger • 2006

# LEGO® PIRATES

The LEGO® Pirates theme made its debut in 1989 and featured Captain Redbeard with his crew of swashbucklers sailing the Seven Seas on the Black Sea Barracuda and the Skull's Eye Schooner. The bloodthirsty pirates chased treasure and took on the Imperial Guards, led by Governor Broadside.

Captain Redbeard has a pet monkey called Spinoza

Wooden leg

**Captain Redbeard • 1989**

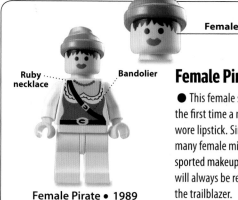

Ruby necklace

Bandolier

Female pirate 1991

## Female Pirate

● This female sailor marked the first time a minifigure wore lipstick. Since then, many female minifigures have sported makeup, but this one will always be remembered as the trailblazer.

**Female Pirate • 1989**

## Armed and Dangerous

● The pirate minifigures were the first to have multiple facial expressions. These swarthy buccaneers sported beards, wore eye patches, and frowned. They also had peg legs and hook hands, which marked the first time that the minifigures' appendages changed from the classic design.

**Pirate • 1994**

**Pirate • 1995**

**DID YOU KNOW?**

The average pirate minifigure, without hair, a sword, or a tri-cornered hat, weighs just a tenth of an ounce!

**Pirate • 1996**

## The Good Guys

● Loosely based on the French and British naval seaman, these minifigures were first known as Imperial Soldiers, then Imperial Guards, and, finally, the Imperial Armada. Though their name changed, they were always the pirates' mortal enemies.

Imperial Guard • 1992

Imperial Guard Admiral • 1995

Imperial Guard Officer • 1992

## Meet the Pirates

● During the 20 years this line has been in existence, there have been over 60 different pirate sets that have included over two dozen different pirate minifigures, as well as crocodiles, parrots, and sharks!

Pirate Blue Shirt • 1991

Pirate • 1991

Pirate • 1996

Skeleton • 1996

Royal feathered hat

King Kuahka • 1994

Female Islander • 1994

## Islanders

● Introduced in 1994, the Islanders inhabited Enchanted Island and the Forbidden Cove, and were independent of the pirates and the imperials, taking both prisoner.

Horned crown

Face paint

Male Islander • 1994

Musket

Tri-cornered
hat with plume

Soldier 1 • 2009

Governor • 2009

# Soldiers

● Led by the Admiral, these brave soldiers of the Royal Navy never give up. Armed with muskets and flintlock pistols, they attack the pirates' ship, Brickbeard's Bounty, before attempting to raid the pirates' secret hideout on a remote island. When they get lucky and actually capture some pirates, they throw them in the prison back at their fort.

**Flintock pistol**

**Epaulets**

Pirate Skeleton • 2009

Soldier 3 • 2009

Captain Brickbeard • 2009

## Pirates

● Captain Brickbeard took over from Captain Redbeard in 2009. He appears in three sets from 2009 and still has his pet monkey, Spinoza.

**Spyglass**

Soldier 2 • 2009

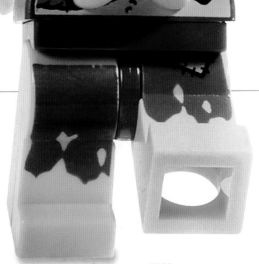

Male Pirate 1 • 2009

Male Pirate 2 • 2009

Male Pirate 3 • 2009

Female Pirate • 2009

Male Pirate 4 • 2009

Castaway • 2009

Male Pirate 5 • 2009

# LEGO® ADVENTURERS

This theme was first released in 1998 and consists of four sub-themes. They all follow Australian explorer and archaeologist Johnny Thunder's travels from Egypt to the Amazon, from Dino Island to the Orient, in his quest for ancient artefacts and adventure. Johnny Thunder tries get to prized antiquities before his archrivals, Baron von Barron and Slyboot.

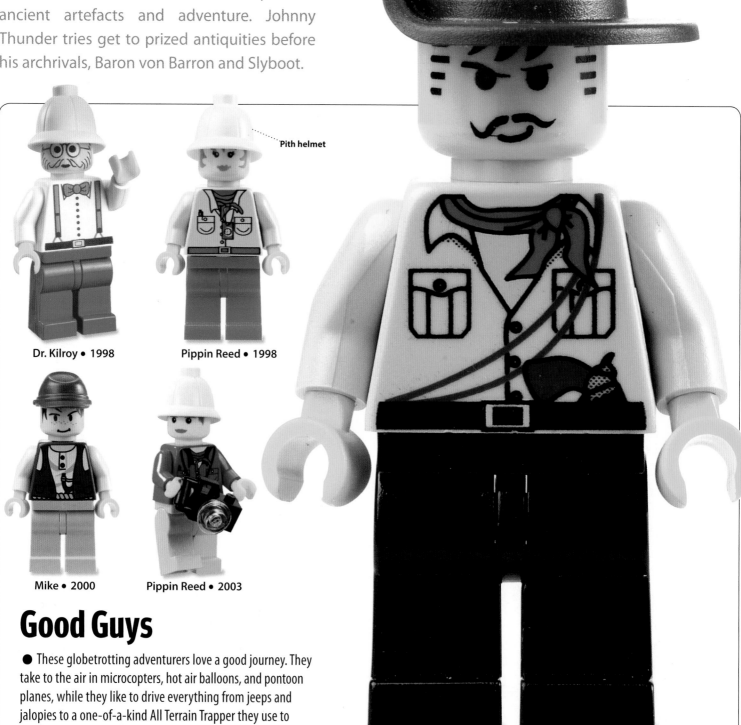

Pith helmet

**Dr. Kilroy • 1998**

**Pippin Reed • 1998**

**Mike • 2000**

**Pippin Reed • 2003**

Johnny Thunder 1 • 2003

## Good Guys

● These globetrotting adventurers love a good journey. They take to the air in microcopters, hot air balloons, and pontoon planes, while they like to drive everything from jeeps and jalopies to a one-of-a-kind All Terrain Trapper they use to capture Prehistoric beasts on Dino Island.

## Egyptian Desert

● This is the first of the adventurers sub-themes and was released in 1998. It follows Johnny Thunder's adventures in the Egyptian desert to find the magical ruby Re-Gou.

Pharoah Skeleton 1 • 1998

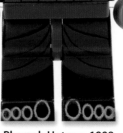

Pharoah Hotep • 1998

Pharoah Skeleton 2 • 1998

Baron Von Barron • 1998

Baron Von Barron • 1998

Lord Sam Sinister • 1998

**DID YOU KNOW?**
LEGOLAND® California has a Land of Adventure, where you can see a giant LEGO® pharaoh made out of 300,000 bricks.

Mr. Cunningham • 2000

---

## Jungle Adventure

● Thunder travels to the Amazonian Jungle to find the the famous Sun Disc. This sub-theme introduces new bad guys, Señor Palomar and Rudo Villano. Achu, the keeper of the ancient treasures, and a spider with web were also new additions.

Achu's cape is brightly patterned on the back

Gabarros • 1999

Senor Palomar • 1999

Rudo Villano • 1999

Achu • 1999

Alexis is from the Dino Island sub-theme

Alexis Sinister • 2000

Dr. Kilroy 1 • 2003

**Flying helmet with goggles**

Pippin Reed 1 • 2003

Johnny Thunder 2 • 2003

## Orient Expedition

● Released in 2003, this was the fourth LEGO® Adventurers theme. It is set around Johnny Thunder's adventures in India, China, and Mount Everest.

Dr. Kilroy 2 • 2003

Pippin Reed 2 • 2003

Johnny Thunder 3 • 2003

Babloo • 2003

Jing Lee • 2003

**Snow shoes**

**Backpack with pickax**

Sangye Dorje • 2003

Baron Von Barron • 2003

Palace Guard • 2003

Maharaja Lallu • 2003

Ngan Pa • 2003

Dragon Fortress Guards • 2003

Guardian Head 2003

Dragon Fortress Guardian • 2003

Emperor Chang Wu • 2003

# The Bad Guys

● No matter where Johnny Thunder goes, he is always dodging bullets, crossbow bolts, and sword swipes from a variety of villains. Whether it's Lord Sam Sinister at the Mummy's Tomb or Maharaha Lallu at the Scorpion's Palace, evil lurks around every corner.

# LEGO® VIKINGS

Introduced in 2005, these fierce Nordic warriors sail the Seven Seas in search of adventure. Along the way, they battle fearsome creatures—mostly from Norse mythology—like the Fafnir Dragon, Fenris Wolf, and Midgard Serpent. The vikings also starred in their own one-of-a-kind chess set, which pitted the red Vikings against their blue counterparts.

These helmets were new for the vikings theme. They had new horn pieces rather than reusing the ones from 1994's Islanders sets

Viking King 1 • 2005

Viking King 2 • 2005

## Noble Norsemen

● Whether he's captaining the longboat or lording over his fortress, the Viking King is a fearless leader and a daunting opponent. You can always pick him out on the battlefield because he wears an eyecatching golden helmet and wields a giant broadsword.

Viking King 1 • 2005

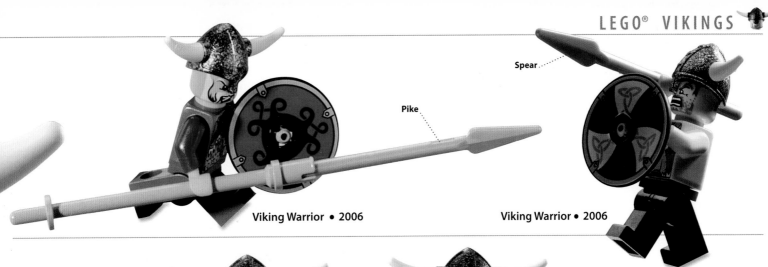

Spear

Pike

Viking Warrior • 2006

Viking Warrior • 2006

Seven vikings sets were introduced over two years. The battleax blades later appeared in Dwarves sets from 2007's LEGO® Castle theme.

Viking Warrior 1 • 2005

Breastplate

Viking Warrior 2 • 2005

## Formidable Fighters

● Dressed in pieces of armor they have stolen from their defeated enemies, these Viking Warriors are a motley crew. Armed with everything from pikes and spears to swords and axs, they bravely defend their village from monsters.

Helmet with noseguard

Viking Warrior 3 • 2005

Viking Warrior 4 • 2005

Viking Warrior 5 • 2006

Viking Warrior • 2005

Viking Warrior • 2005

Viking Warrior • 2005

Viking Warrior • 2005

The Skeleton from LEGO® Castle was the first minifigure to have its own unique body. It was followed by many more, including robots, aliens, rock monsters, and others.

Thunder Driller • 2009

# LEGO® SPACE

Launched in 1978, LEGO® Space is one of the richest themes in minifigure history, spawning a myriad of sub-themes like LEGO Mars Mission and LEGO Space Police. No matter where in the solar system the astronauts are, they come armed to the teeth with ray guns, bazookas, and laser armed jetpacks. And even though the theme has evolved over time, you can still find the original logo of a spaceship rocketing around a golden planet on the spacesuit of the Mars Mission team if you look closely.

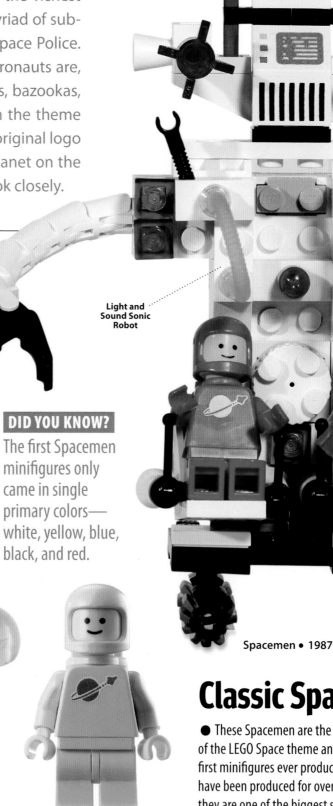

**Light and Sound Sonic Robot**

**DID YOU KNOW?**
The first Spacemen minifigures only came in single primary colors—white, yellow, blue, black, and red.

Spacemen • 1987

## Classic Space

● These Spacemen are the original stars of the LEGO Space theme and some of the first minifigures ever produced. Since they have been produced for over 30 years, they are one of the biggest selling minifigures in the LEGO Group's history.

Spaceman • 1979

Spaceman • 1979

## LEGO® Space Police

● Once Blacktron had been declared "bad guys", the LEGO space policemen were introduced to defend Futuron from them. Nearly all the LEGO Space Police vehicles come with a jail cell containing a Blacktron prisoner.

## Insectoids

● The Insectoids are insectoid cyborgs, some of which have wings and legs like insects. This was the third LEGO Space theme to have a female minifigure.

**Insectoid • 1998**

**Blacktron 1 • 1987**

**Space Policeman • 1992**

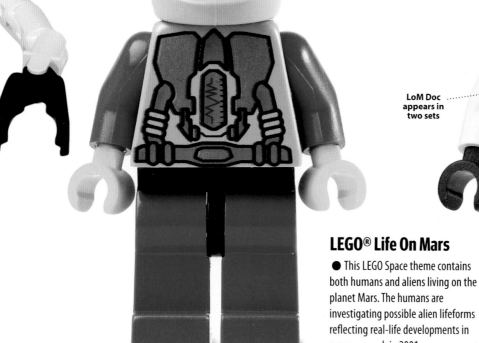

**LoM Doc** appears in two sets

## LEGO® Life On Mars

● This LEGO Space theme contains both humans and aliens living on the planet Mars. The humans are investigating possible alien lifeforms reflecting real-life developments in space research in 2001.

**Assistant • 2001**

**LoM Doc• 2001**

**Canopus • 2001**

**Altair • 2001**

**Vega • 2001**

**Pollux • 2001**

**Martian • 2001**

# LEGO® Mars Mission

● Earth needed energy, so the astronaut crew blasted off to seek it out on the red planet of Mars. Luckily, they went heavily armed, because they got an unwelcome reception from the aliens who live there. Looks like that MX-11 Astro Fighter is going to come in handy!

Astronaut • 2007

Astronaut • 2007

Astronaut • 2007

Astronaut • 2007

Astronaut • 2007

Astronaut • 2007

Alien • 2007

Alien Commander • 2008

Crystal detector

Mini-Robot • 2008

Biff Starling • 2002

Sandy is one of only four female minifigures from the LEGO Space theme

Sandy Moondust • 2002

**DID YOU KNOW?**

In 2003, minifigures went interplanetary when pictures of Sandy and Biff minifigures were shot into space on board the Mars Rover.

## Space Police III

● The LEGO Space Police sub-theme has had three incarnations, in 1989, 1992, and 2009. The latest version finds our courageous cosmic cops busting alien crooks who are dead set on stealing gold bars and big bucks.

Space Policeman • 2009

Space Policeman • 2009

Space Policeman • 2009

Space Policeman and Skull Twin 1 • 2009

Space Policeman • 2009

### DID YOU KNOW?

The LEGO Space sets were some of the first to feature specially molded LEGO pieces, which gave the rockets and moon buggies a more futuristic and streamlined look.

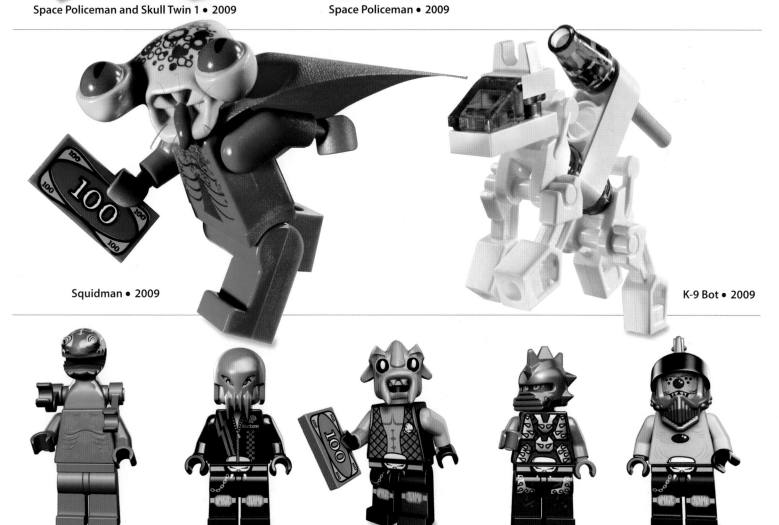

Squidman • 2009

K-9 Bot • 2009

Frenzy • 2009

Skull Twin 2 • 2009

Kranxx • 2009

Slizer • 2009

Snake • 2009

# LEGO® AGENTS

LEGO® Agents have just one goal: Stop the nefarious Dr. Inferno and his evil henchmen. Their missions against these diabolical criminals take them all over the world, from snowy mountains to steamy jungles and oceans teeming with cyborg sharks. Luckily, they've got all sorts of high-tech machines to help them out, including jetpacks, turbocars, and supersonic jets.

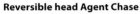
**Reversible head Agent Chase**

**Agent Swipe • 2009**

## Super Spies

● These agents have got an endless supply of secret skills and super-spy gadgets, so they're unstoppable, no matter what environment you put them in. They can even take down glow-in-the-dark octopuses and remote-controlled crocodiles.

**Agent Chase • 2008**

**Zipline pulley**

**Agent Swift • 2009**

**Agent Trace • 2008**

**Agent Fuse • 2008**

**Agent Charge • 2008**

Henchman • 2008

Fire Arm • 2008

Claw-Dette • 2008

# Bad to the Bone

● This wicked crew of evildoers has a nonstop vendetta against the Agents. Dr. Inferno even built a gigantic laser cannon on top of his hidden volcano base that he wants to use to rid the world of the LEGO Agents once and for all.

Gold Tooth • 2008

Dina-Mite • 2009

Dr. D. Zaster • 2009

Dr. Inferno • 2008

Dollar Bill • 2009

Break Jaw • 2008

Harpoon gun

Slime Face • 2008

Saw Fist • 2008

Spy Clops • 2008

# LEGO® DINO ATTACK

Launched in 2005, LEGO® Dino Attack is set in 2010 when dinosaurs have appeared again on Earth. The sets feature amazing futuristic vehicles that battle with fearsome dinosaurs. Luckily, the LEGO Dino Attack team is equipped with weapons like Voltaic Launchers and Quintronic Beam Emitters.

Binoculars

Vest with bullets and knife

Digger • 2005

Digger • 2005

Digger • 2005

## Renaissance Man

● Digger is a paleontologist, a marksman, and a daredevil all wrapped in one. He likes to test his luck when he battles the dinosaurs, often waiting until the last possible moment before zapping them with the Cosmotronic Ray.

### Rad Scientist
● Inventor of the Xenon Multi-Mode Launcher, Specs is the techie and scientist of the team. He is conflicted about their battle with the dinosaurs, preferring to capture them for study instead.

**Specs • 2005**

Abseil rope

Camouflage pattern

**Shadow • 2005**

**DID YOU KNOW?**
This theme is referred to as LEGO Dino Attack in the United States, Australia, and Japan, but it is known as LEGO Dino 2010 in Europe.

**Shadow • 2005**

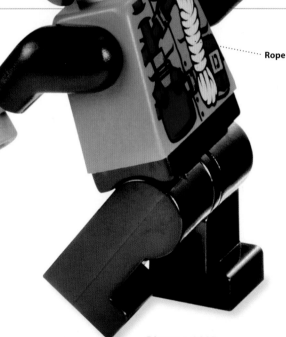

Rope

**Digger • 2005**

**T-Rex • 2005**

**Viper • 2005**          **Viper • 2005**

### Toothsome Terror
● With a mouth that's a nuclear furnace, incredible strength, and near invulnerability, the T-Rex is an imposing opponent. With one sweep of its tail it can take down a building, and with a bite of its massive jaws it can sheer through a steel girder like it was butter.

# LEGO® AQUAZONE

Deep in the blue underworld of the Bermuda Triangle lies hidden a sunken treasure. It is submerged in the most perilous stretch of ocean in the world, so it takes truly brave souls to rise to that watery challenge. That is where the LEGO® Aqua Raiders come in. Introduced in 2007 and armed with state-of-the-art weaponry and submersibles, these daring divers are ready to take on anything in their pursuit of gold coins, crystals, and diamonds.

### Aqua Royalty

● The Raiders found this skeletal king inside a shipwreck, where he still guarded his treasure of gold coins, diamonds and golden platters. This monarch can't lift a finger against intruders, so divers should keep an eye out for poisonous sea snakes.

Skeleton King • 2007

## Brave Divers

● With a forked trident emblazoned on their wet suits, the LEGO Aqua Raiders are ready to go down to any depth to pursue treasure. These daring divers arm themselves with spear guns and harpoon cannons because they never know what kinds of aquatic enemies they'll find themselves facing off against.

Aqua Raider Diver 1 • 2007

Aqua Raider Diver 2 • 2007

Aqua Raider Diver 3 • 2007

Aquanaut 1 • 1995

Aquanaut 2 • 1995

## DID YOU KNOW?

Aquazone was the first LEGO theme to be introduced with more than one sub-theme. When it came out in 1985 it included both the Aquanauts and the Aquasharks.

Aquashark 1 • 1996

Aquashark 2 • 1996

Stingray 1 • 1998

Stingray 2 • 1998

Stingray 3 • 1998

Hydronaut 1 • 1998

Hydronaut 2 • 1998

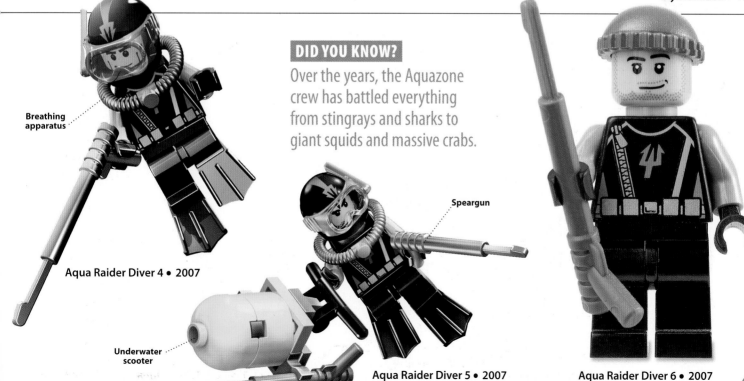

**Breathing apparatus**

Aqua Raider Diver 4 • 2007

## DID YOU KNOW?

Over the years, the Aquazone crew has battled everything from stingrays and sharks to giant squids and massive crabs.

**Speargun**

**Underwater scooter**

Aqua Raider Diver 5 • 2007

Aqua Raider Diver 6 • 2007

# UNDERGROUND

LEGO® Rock Raiders was launched in 1999. Almost a decade later, the Underground theme was revived with LEGO Power Miners, which borrowed ideas like energy crystals and Rock Monsters from the earlier sets.

Axel • 1999

Axel • 2000

Driver gear

**DID YOU KNOW?**

Though LEGO Rock Raiders sets were only produced in 1999 and 2000, the theme inspired a slew of spin-offs, including comic books, video games, and graphic novels.

Bandit • 1999

Jet • 1999

Sparks • 1999

## LEGO® Rock Raiders

● These hardy miners make up the crew of the LMS Explorer. This spaceship is damaged when it's accidentally flown into asteroid field and then sucked through a wormhole to a parallel universe. There LEGO Rock Raiders land on Planet U in hopes of collecting mysterious Energy Crystals, which they will use to power their ship and fly home. If they can only evade the Rock Monsters, they just might make it back to their galaxy alive.

Docs • 1999

Captain uniform

Chief • 2000

### LEGO® Power Miners

● Earth is being invaded from the inside out. Mystifying Rock Monsters are tunneling below the surface in search of energy crystals and causing strange earthquakes in the process, so it's up to the Power Miners to stop them. Luckily, they've got underground machines like the Claw Digger and the Thunder Driller to help them out.

Power Miner 1 • 2009

Power Miner 2 • 2009

Power Miner 3 • 2009

**Handheld driller**

Power Miner 5 • 2009

### DID YOU KNOW?

The Rock Monsters star in their own online game called Rock Rocket, where players burrow deep below the surface of the earth into hidden caves on a quest to chomp crystals.

Power Miner 4 • 2009

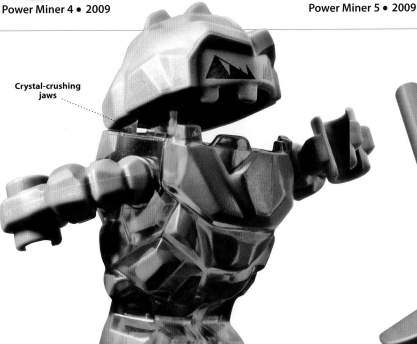

**Crystal-crushing jaws**

Boulderax • 2009

**Energy crystal**

Power Miner 6 • 2009

Firox • 2009

Glaciator • 2009

Meltrox • 2009

Sulfurix • 2009

# LEGO® ALPHA TEAM

These hardworking heroes made their debut in 2001 before setting off on Mission Deep Sea in 2002 and Mission Deep Freeze in 2004. On land, under water, or in the depths of the Artic, they're always battling Ogel, a sinister scoundrel with seemingly unlimited resources and an enthusiasm for evildoing.

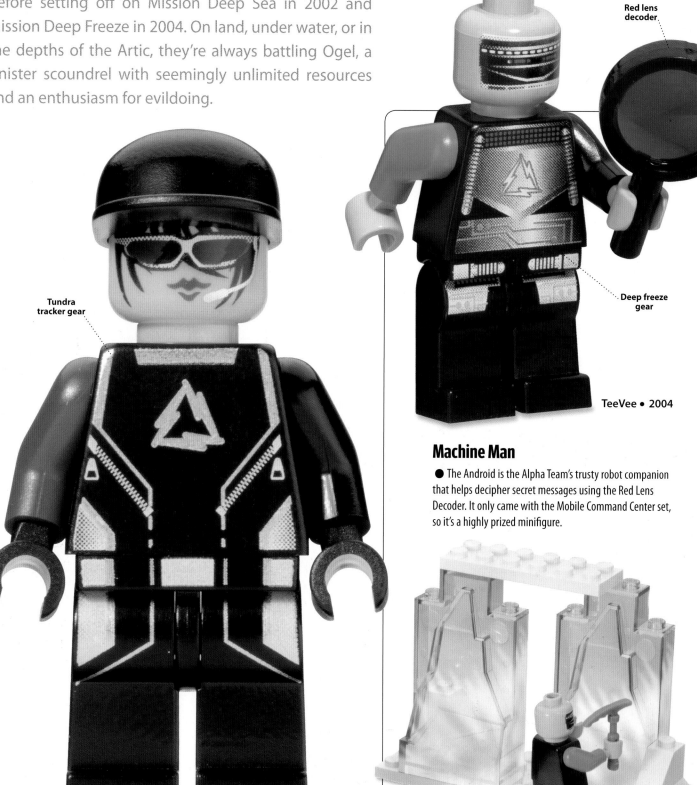

Red lens decoder

Deep freeze gear

TeeVee • 2004

Tundra tracker gear

Radia • 2004

### Machine Man

● The Android is the Alpha Team's trusty robot companion that helps decipher secret messages using the Red Lens Decoder. It only came with the Mobile Command Center set, so it's a highly prized minifigure.

TeeVee • 2004

## Mission Deep Freeze

● For this dangerous assignment, the Alpha Team must journey to Antarctica to stop Ogel, who plans on using his ice orbs to freeze time itself. Commanding the Chill Speeder and the Blizzard Blaster, the Alpha Team has to uncover Ogel's hidden base before time runs out.

Zed • 2005

Diamond • 2004

Flex • 2004

Deep freeze gear

Alpha Team logo

Dash • 2004

Charge • 2004

Arrow • 2004

Arctic helmet

Ice orb

Super Ice Drone • 2005

Ogel Minion • 2004

Hook hand

Ogel • 2004

# Cold-hearted Crook

● Ogel is a classic supervillain bent on conquering the world. With the help of his evil orbs and an army of mindless drones, he is determined to enslave humanity. According to designers, he is a descendent of evil Lord Vladek from the LEGO® KNIGHTS' KINGDOM™ theme.

# LEGO® EXO-FORCE™

Deep in a jungle lies Sentai Mountain, where war is being waged. The LEGO® EXO-FORCE™ team is locked in a life-or-death battle against the robots, who rose up against their human masters. Led by Keiken, these brightly-topped rebels joined the LEGO universe in 2006 and feature reversible heads to show a fighting face as well as their standard face.

Hikaru • 2007

## Hikaru

● This cool and collected commander got his start as a "robot buster," a test driver for new machines. Now he's a top-notch pilot and a marksman who never misses.

Hikaru fighting face 2006

### DID YOU KNOW?

The EXO-FORCE™ theme was inspired by the popular Japanese manga genre known as mecha, which revolves around giant battle machines controlled by humans.

Hikaru • 2006

Keiken fighting face 2006

## Sensei Keiken

● This sage leader founded the LEGO EXO-FORCE universe and built the first battle machines to fight the robots. Ironically, he is also the designer of the first robot to rebel against the humans.

Sensei Keiken • 2006

Ha-ya-to • 2006

Ha-ya-to • 2007

## Ha-ya-to

● A daredevil with a great sense of humor, Ha-ya-to is a nonstop risk-taker. An incredibly skilled pilot, he would always rather be in the air fighting robots than hanging back on the ground.

Hitomi • 2007

Supernova gear

Takeshi • 2006

Grand titan gear

Takeshi • 2006

## Takeshi

● Takeshi is not one of those guys you want to get in a fight with. He's intense and powerful, so it's lucky for his teammates that all his aggression is focused on their robot enemies.

Blade titan gear

Takeshi • 2007

## Hitomi

● The lone female in the EXO-FORCE theme, Hitomi has a background in mechanics, but she would much rather be exercising her skills as a martial artist or an accomplished pilot.

Uplink gear

Ryo (with standard and fighting faces) • 2006

**DID YOU KNOW?**

The LEGO EXO-FORCE™ team was the first set of minifigures to feature brightly-colored rubber hairpieces.

## Ryo

● The geek of the group, Ryo is a technical wunderkind. He was one of the whiz kids who designed the EXO-FORCE™ battle machines and he knows how to fix anything and everything.

Camouflage gearr

Ryo • 2007

Gate Guard • 2006

Pincer hands

Iron Drone • 2006

# Robots

● Cold, cruel, and cunning, these are the EXO-FORCE archenemies. They have varying degrees of artificial intelligence, but are all very dangerous. The Iron Drone's method is always "charge straight ahead and break things," while the Devastators formulate plots and react on-the-fly.

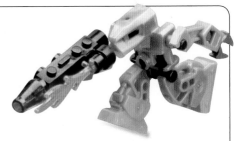

Meca One • 2006

Devastator • 2006

Devastator (Blue) • 2006

Devastator (Green) • 2006

Devastator (Red) • 2006

# LEGO® SOCCER

In 2000 LEGO® Soccer was the first LEGO® Sports theme to be released. LEGO® NBA, LEGO Gravity Games (featuring snowboarders and skateboarders), and LEGO® Hockey followed in 2003. LEGO Soccer (or LEGO® Football as it was named in some countries) is the largest theme with over 25 sets released.

Red team goalkeeper jersey

Goalkeepers have black hands to look like goalie gloves

Red Team Goalkeeper • 2001

Red Team jersey

Red Team 1 • 2001

Red Team 2 • 2001

## Perfect Pitch

● The LEGO Soccer theme sets feature stickers, giving fans a chance to choose one of five LEGO Soccer teams. On the stadiums there are special bases allowing builders to aim and "kick" the ball.

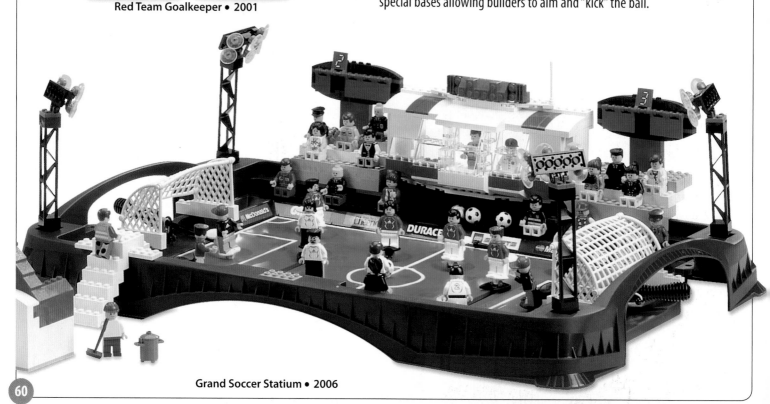

Grand Soccer Statium • 2006

Blue Team 1 • 2001

Blue Team 2 • 2001

Blue Team 3 • 2001

Blue Team Goalkeeper • 2001

Blue Team jersey

Blue team goalkeeper jersey

## The Beautiful Game

● The LEGO Soccer Mania video game has an Adventure mode so you can play against teams made up of minifigures from across the themes, such as pirates, martians, and skeletons.

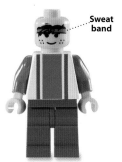
Red and Blue Team 1 • 2001

Sweat band

Red and Blue Team 2 • 2001

Green and White Team 1 •

Green and White Team 2 •

Red Team 3 • 2001

LEGO® *Star Wars*™ was the first intellectual property to be licensed in LEGO Group history. Since then, there have been LEGO® sets introduced that are based on Indiana Jones, Batman, and Harry Potter, as well as sports teams.

Jabba's Sail Barge™ • 2006

# LEGO® *STAR WARS*™

Not so long ago, in a galaxy not so far away at all…

When LEGO® *Star Wars*™ minifigures started hitting shelves in 1999, they were the first ever licensed LEGO characters. Since then minifigures from *The Phantom Menace* through *Return of the Jedi* and *The Clone Wars* have been released. It doesn't matter if the minifigures are on the side of the Alliance or the Empire— they're some of the coolest the LEGO Group has ever produced.

Anakin Skywalker™ • 1999

Holoprojector

R2-D2™ • 1999

Padmé Amidala™ • 1999

Jar Jar Binks™ • 1999

### DID YOU KNOW?
Jar Jar Binks was the first minifigure to have a specially molded head.

Obi-Wan Kenobi™ • 2005

This Anakin minifigure has short legs

Anakin Skywalker™ • 2007

Battle Droid Pilot • 2007

This droid was the first to have a turned hand for holding a blaster

Battle Droid • 2005

Battle Droid • 2007

### Men of Steel
● Battle droids are the cannon fodder of the Trade Federation Droid Army. Since they are flimsy, slow-to-react, and somewhat stupid, they rely on their sheer numbers to defeat their enemies.

Darth Maul™ • 2000

Qui-Gon Jinn™ • 1999

Battle Droid Commander • 2000

Watto™ • 2001

Destroyer Droid • 2002

Pit Droid • 1999

# Episode II

## Two-Faced Killer

● Zam Wessel is a shape-shifting bounty hunter from the planet Zolan. In her true form, she is a green-skinned reptile, but she usually appears as a red-haired woman.

Geonosian Battle Droid • 2003

Winged Geonosian™ •

Tusken Raider™ • 2002

Zam Wessel™ • 2002

## Ruling Class

● The winged Geonosians are the elite of their society. They rule harshly over the wingless Geonosians, forcing them to work long hours, often in dangerous conditions.

Geonosian™ • 2003

Anakin Skywalker™ • 2002

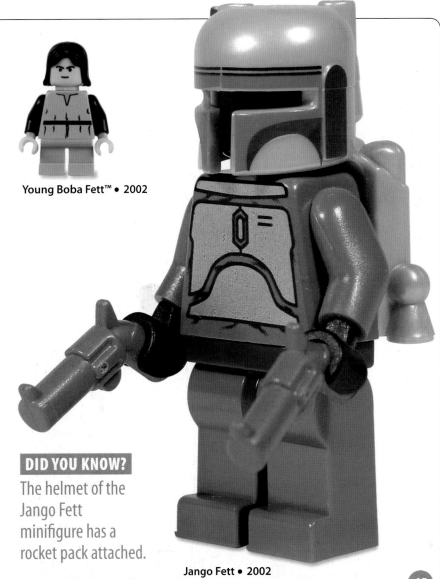

Young Boba Fett™ • 2002

Super Battle Droid • 2002

Obi-Wan Kenobi™ • 2002

## Super Sized fighters

● Super battle droids are similar to regular battle droids, but are larger and stronger. They also have a toughened armor that protects their working parts from damage.

Count Dooku™ • 2002

Jango Fett • 2002

Mace Windu™ • 2005

Luminara Unduli™ • 2005

### Jedi Master
● This Mirialan Jedi Master is a force to be reckoned with. She is highly skilled when it comes to lightsaber dueling, and she is also extremely flexible and agile, making it impossible for enemies to pin her down.

## Episode III
### Water Wonder
● Kit Fisto is an amphibious Jedi, who is even more powerful underwater than he is on land. He can wield water as a weapon using the Force and his specially designed lightsaber is waterproof.

Kit Fisto™ • 2007

General Grievous™ • 2005

General Grievous • 2007

### DID YOU KNOW?
The oval on the ammo halter of the Wookiee Warrior minifigure contains an emblem of his clan.

Wookiee Warrior™ • 2005

Obi-Wan Kenobi™ • 2007

MagnaDroid™ • 2008

## Changing Sides

● Anakin Skywalker is manipulated into turning against the Jedi by the evil Sith lord Darth Sideous. The former Jedi knight goes over to the dark side, becoming an apprentice to Sideous and taking the name Darth Vader. He follows Sith orders to destroy the Jedi, even fighting with his friend Obi-Wan Kenobi.

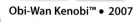

Anakin Skywalker™ • 2005

Battle scars

Anakin Skywalker™ • 2005

Darth Vader™ • 2005

# Clones

## Multiple copies

● Clone troopers are all created from the DNA of just one person—bounty hunter Jango Fett. The Clone Army fought for the Republic in the Clone Wars, which lasted over 300 years.

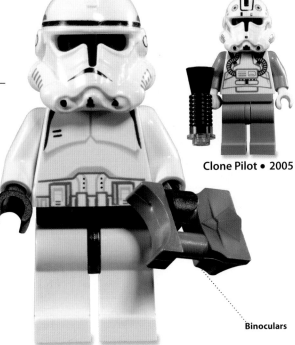

Clone Pilot • 2005

Clone Pilot • 2008

Clone Trooper • 2005

Binoculars

### DID YOU KNOW?
The earlier clone minifigures had blank heads, because facial features were not visible under their helmets.

Clone Trooper • 2005

Captain Rex • 2008

Clone Recon Trooper • 2005

Aerial Clone Trooper • 2005

Clone Trooper • 2005

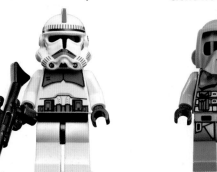
Clone Gunner • 2009   Shock Trooper • 2007

Scout Trooper • 2005

# Hired Guns

● Dressed identically in plastoid armor, Stormtroopers are the muscle of the Empire. The rank-and-file troopers have a white uniform while specialist troopers have adapted battle dress.

Stormtrooper • 2002

Stormtrooper • 2006

Sandtrooper • 2007

Snowtrooper • 2003

TIE Interceptor Pilot • 2007

## Shady Characters

● Shadow Troopers are a unit of clones developed specially for undercover work. Their armor contains magnetic plates that can altar their appearance, enabling them to infiltrate enemy facilites.

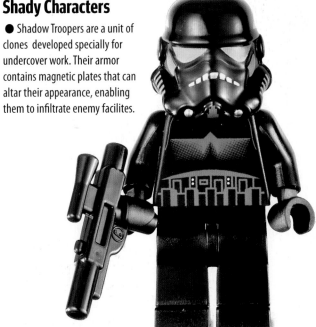
Shadow Trooper • 2007

# Episode IV
## Lord of the Sith

● Darth Vader's specially designed suit serves both as armor and as housing for a the life support system he needs after almost being burned to death during his duel with Obi-Wan Kenobi.

Darth Vader™ • 2000

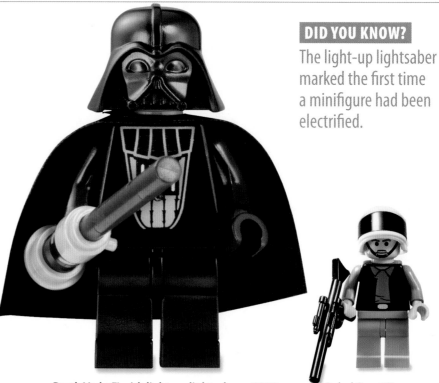

**DID YOU KNOW?**
The light-up lightsaber marked the first time a minifigure had been electrified.

Imperial Officer • 2006

Grand Moff Tarkin™ • 2006

Darth Vader™ with light-up lightsaber • 2005

Rebel Scout Trooper • 2008

Luke Skywalker™ • 1999

Han Solo™ • 2004

**DID YOU KNOW?**
There have been ten different Han Solo minifigures released since the first, in 2000.

Han Solo™ • 2000

Obi-Wan Kenobi™ • 2004

## Future Jedi

● Until he saw Princess Leia's holographic message, Luke Skywalker thought he was doomed to a life of farming. Then he met Obi-Wan Kenobi and set off on an intergalactic adventure that would change his world forever.

Dack ™• 2004

Greedo™ • 2004

Greedo is very rare. He was only released in Benelux

Luke Skywalker™ • 2004

Chewbacca™ • 2005

R2-D5™ • 2006

Rebel Pilot • 2007

C-3PO™ • 2000

# Episode V
## Smooth Operator

● Lando Calrissian may have lost the *Millennium Falcon™* to Han Solo in a sabacc game, but he's usually one sly fox. He aids Leia, Chewbacca and the droids in their escape from Darth Vader's clutches, then rescues Luke from the underbelly of Cloud City.

Lando Calrissian™ • 2003

Hoth Gear

Princess Leia™ • 2004

Han Solo™ • 2004

**DID YOU KNOW?**
LEGO *Star Wars* was one of the first themes to utilize realistic skin colors on its minifigures, which is why some older minifigures are classic yellow and some have flesh tones.

Gimer stick

Bespin Guard • 2006

R5-D4/Astromech Droid™ • 2007

Lobot™ • 2002

**DID YOU KNOW?**
The Yoda minifigure was the first to be a different height, which designers accomplished by shortening his legs.

K-3PO™ • 2007

Rebel Soldier • 2009

Yoda™ • 2009

# Bounty Hunters

● In *Episode V: The Empire Strikes Back*, Darth Vader hires the galaxy's most ruthless bounty hunters. Their mission is to track down the *Millennium Falcon* for a substantial reward. Dengar and IG-88 were unsuccessful, but Boba Fett succeeded where they had failed. He followed the *Millennium Falcon* to Cloud City and when Han was frozen in carbonite, Boba transported him to Jabba the Hutt's palace to collect his bounty.

Boba Fett™ • 2006

Blaster gun

Dengar ™• 2006

**DID YOU KNOW?**
Boba Fett wears a Mitrinomon Z-6 jet pack with a missile launcher built into its top.

IG-88 ™• 2006

**Force pike**

**Black glove**

Emperor's Royal Guard • 2006

Luke Skywalker™ • 2002

**Scarred face**

Darth Vader™ • 2006

Darth Vader™ • 2008

**Breathing apparatus**

Darth Vader™ • 2008

## Episode VI

### Red Devils

● The Emperor's Royal Guards are an elite force who accompany Emperor Palpatine wherever he goes. Though they all carry force pikes, they are trained in a variety of weapons and martial arts.

Bib Fortuna™ • 2003

**Goblet**

R2-D2™ • 2006

Luke Skywalker™ • 2002

Wicket W. Warrick™ • 2009

Lando Calrissian™ • 2006

### Imprisoned Princess

● When Leia shows up at Jabba the Hutt's palace disguised as Boushh the bounty hunter, she almost tricks the green gangster. But she's busted and forced into slavery, not to mention a metal bikini.

Ten Numb™ • 2006

Admiral Ackbar™ • 2009

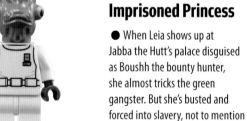

Jabba the Hutt ™• 2003

**Vibro-ax**

Gamorrean Guard • 2006

Princess Leia ™• 2006

Tattoo

Hondo Ohnaka™ • 2009

## The Clone Wars

### Double Trouble

● Dark Jedi Ventress wields dual red lightsabers like her mentor Count Dooku. In The *Clone Wars* film, Ventress' lightsabers join together at the hilt to form a deadly double blade.

Turk Falso™• 2009

Count Dooku™ • 2009

Nute Gunray™ • 2009

Asajj Ventress™ • 2008

Palpatine™ • 2009

Onaconda Farr™ • 2009

Plo Koon™ • 2008

Mace Windu™ • 2009

Montrals

Rotta the Huttlet

Ahsoka™ • 2008

Anakin Skywalker™ • 2008

### Ahsoka Tano

● Ahsoka Tano is Anakin Skywalker's young Padawan learner. One of her first missions is to retrieve Rotta (Jabba the Hutt's baby son) from a dastardly kidnapping plot, carried out by the Sith.

Commander Cody™ • 2008

Obi-Wan Kenobi™ • 2008

RY-AY™ • 2009

Yoda™ • 2009

# LEGO® SPIDER-MAN™

Based on the first two blockbuster *Spider-Man*™ films, many of these minifigures started out in the LEGO® Studios theme which was released in 2000. Spider-Man minifigures are some of the most popular characters to feature in fans' stop animation videos, which are known as brickfilms.

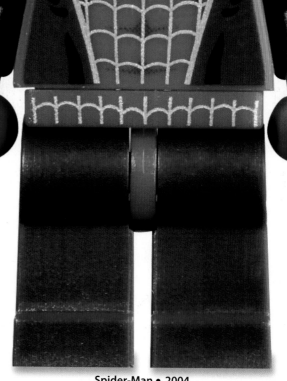

Spider-Man also comes with a neck bracket so he can be studk to walls.

Two of the three Peter Parker minifigures that have been released wear glasses.

Peter Parker • 2004

## DID YOU KNOW?

When a radioactive arachnid bit Peter Parker, he developed superhuman strength, the power to cling to walls, and a special spider-sense that alerts him to danger.

Spider-Man • 2004

Spider-Man • 2004

## Alter Ego

● When he's not fighting crime in New York City as a wall-crawling superhero, Peter Parker works as a photographer for the *Daily Bugle*. Ironically, his biggest accomplishment as a journalist is snapping pictures of Spider-Man!

## Near and Dear

● Mary Jane is Peter Parker's friend and confidant, not to mention the love of his life. It's too bad that she keeps getting caught up in Spider-Man's troubles, because the web-slinger constantly has to rescue her from certain death.

Aunt May • 2004

J. Jonah Jameson • 2004

Mary Jane • 2004

Ambulance Driver • 2004

Police Officer • 2004

Security Guard 1 • 2004

Security Guard 2 • 2004

Doc Ock 2004

Doc Ock 2004

**Titanium tentacles**

## Four-Armed and Dangerous

● Otto Gunther Octavius was just another mad scientist until a freak accident fused his mentally controlled tentacles to his torso, turning him into one of Spider-Man's most dangerous foes.

Dr. Ock • 2004

Harry Osborn • 2004

Harry Osborn • 2004

## Spawn of Green Goblin

● Harry Osborn was a dear friend to Peter Parker and Mary Jane, until Spider-Man killed his father. Suddenly, a friend becomes a foe, as the son becomes his father's alter ego and tries to avenge his death.

Jewel Thief 1 • 2004

Jewel Thief 2 • 2004

# LEGO® HARRY POTTER™

The LEGO® Harry Potter™ theme was released in 2001 to coincide with the hit film *Harry Potter and the Philosopher's Stone*. Each new Harry Potter™ movie has brought new minifigures, which have gone from being the classic yellow to the new skin tones with specially molded hair to make them look more realistic.

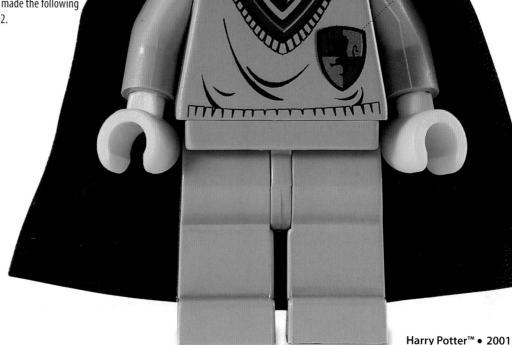

Molded hair

Gryffindor house crest

Harry Potter™ • 2001

### Launching Harry Potter

● A total of fourteen LEGO® Harry Potter™ sets were made for the first movie. To start with, the LEGO Group only produced eleven and three more were made the following year in 2002.

Ron Weasley™ • 2001

Draco Malfoy™ • 2001

## Magic Masters

● These three powerful professors can cast a dazzling array of spells—from Anti-Disapparition Jinxes and Vanishing Spells to Piertotum Locomotor, which brings suits of armor to life!

Dumbledore™ • 2001

Professor Snape™ • 2007

Spell book

Professor McGonagall™ • 2002

Madame Hooch™ • 2002

Goblin • 2002

Draco Malfoy™ • 2002

Harry Potter™ • 2003

Golden Snitch

Quidditch uniform

## Financial Wizards

● Goblins not only run Gringotts Wizarding Bank, they also mint the money. Each of the Galleons, Sickles, and Knuts that they craft is personally stamped with a serial number that identifies the goblin who made it.

Harry Potter™ • 2002

"The oddest thing was seeing myself as a LEGO action figure. It was so strange seeing my cylindrical head." (Daniel Radcliffe)

Professor Trelawney™ • 2004

Dumbledore™ • 2001

## Wild Man

● This Defense Against the Dark Arts professor forgot to take Wolfsbane and transformed into a werewolf. His unique molded wolf's head allows him to change between his animal and human form.

Professor Lupin™ • 2004

Professor Lupin/Werewolf™ • 2004

Professor Snape™ • 2001

Professor Snape Boggart™ • 2004

## School Chums

● These minifigures for Harry, Ron, and Hermione show the characters dressed in their traditional Hogwarts school uniforms that include grey pants, a grey wool sweater, and a maroon and yellow tie that indicates they live in Gryffindor.

Hermione™ • 2004

Draco Malfoy™ in Quidditch Uniform • 2004

Harry Potter™ • 2004

Ron Weasley™ • 2004

Hermione™ • 2004

**DID YOU KNOW?**

Voldemort was the first minifigure to have a glow-in-the-dark head!

Glow-in-the-dark head

Voldemort™ • 2005

Voldemort™ • 2005

Trident

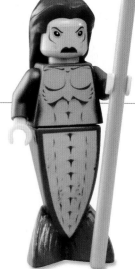

Death Eater • 2005

Lucius Malfoy™ • 2005

Mermaid • 2005

Skeleton • 2005

**DID YOU KNOW?**

The first Harry Potter theme marked the first appearance of a black skeleton in the LEGO universe.

Wormtail™ • 2005

Wormtail™ • 2004

Mad-Eye Moody™ • 2005

Durmstrang school crest

Viktor Krum™ • 2005

Viktor Krum™ • 2005

# Dark Arts

● These two northern European inspired characters are from the Durmstrang Institute, which takes its name from the Spoonerism of the German phrase "Sturm und Drang." Literally translated, this means "storm and stress."

Professor Karkaroff™ • 2005

**Dumbledore™ • 2005**

**Harry Potter™ • 2005**

**Harry Potter™ • 2005**

Flippers

**Harry Potter™ • 2005**

## Triple Vision

● For the release of *Goblet of Fire*, the LEGO Group made three separate Harry Potter figures, which depicted the young magician dressed for adventures on the ground, in the air, and underwater.

**Harry Potter™ • 2007**

**Draco Malfoy™ • 2007**

## Order of the Phoenix

● There was only one Harry Potter set released for Order of the Phoenix—the giant Hogwarts Castle—but it included nine minifigures and two Thestrals. It also marked the first and only appearance of the Dolores Umbridge minifigure.

**Prof. Dolores Umbridge™ • 2007**

**Death Eater • 2007**

**Ron Weasley™ • 2007**

**Hermione™ • 2007**

Bow and arrow

**Hagrid™ • 2007**

**Dumbledore™ • 2007**

**Quirrell™ • 2007**

# LEGO® NBA™

When the LEGO Group drafted the NBA as a new theme in 2003, they wanted to take their game up a notch. So all the kings of the court were made with authentic skin tones and stylized hair. The minifigures came with their own arena, so fans could create their own dream teams and compete in smaller-than-life championships.

Lakers home jersey

Shaquille O'Neal 1 • 2003

NBA Player 1 • 2003

NBA Player 2 • 2003

### Pick-up Artist

● Though a lot of famous NBA stars have their own minifigures, there are also minifigures that represent all the regular ballers who like to go down to their local courts for a pick-up game.

Street Player 1 • 2003

Street Player 2 • 2003

Lakers away jersey

Shaquille O'Neal 2 • 2003

## DID YOU KNOW?

The real life Shaquille O'Neal is over 7 feet tall, weighs 325 pounds and wears size 23 shoes!

Jerry Stackouse • 2003

Pistons jersey

**DID YOU KNOW?**
24 NBA stars joined up to play for the LEGO Group, on more than a dozen teams!

Celtics home jersey

Antoine Walker • 2003

Celtics away jersey

Paul Pierce • 2003

Nets jersey

Jason Kidd • 2003

Mavericks jersey

Steve Nash • 2003

Mavericks jersey

Dirk Nowitzki • 2003

Magic home jersey

Tracy McGrady • 2003

# Spring into Action

● These minifigures are spring-loaded so players can shoot, pass, and even reverse slam dunk. It took a team of four designers and six engineers a full year to develop the arms and hands so the minifigures could hold the basketball and throw it properly.

# LEGO® SPONGEBOB SQUAREPANTS™

Created by former marine biologist Stephen Hillenburg, the hit animated TV show SpongeBob SquarePants™ debuted on Nickelodeon in 1999, though the ocean-dwelling gang didn't join the LEGO® universe until 2006. The colorful cast includes a variety of creatures, from a starfish (Patrick) and a sea snail (Gary) to a Texan squirrel (Sandy Cheeks).

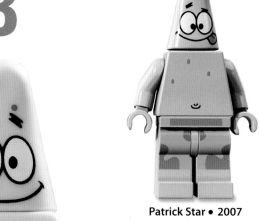

Patrick Star • 2007

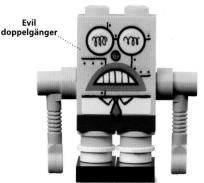

Patrick Star • 2006

SpongeBob SquarePants • 2009

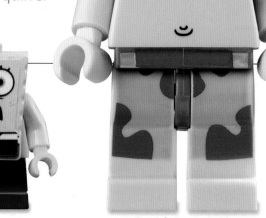

SpongeBob SquarePants • 2007

SpongeBob SquarePants • 2007

SpongeBob SquarePants • 2009

SpongeBob SquarePants • 2006

**Evil doppelgänger**

Robot SpongeBob SquarePants • 2007

## Funny Faces

● He wants to be the best fry cook in the whole ocean, but SpongeBob SquarePants spends more time causing trouble than he does making Krabby Patties. Luckily, he has got a different look for each of his hijinks and adventures.

Gary • 2007

Mr. Krabs • 2006

Mr. Krabs • 2007

Plankton • 2007

**Antenna**

Original head

Modified molded head

Squidward Tentacles • 2006

## Nasty Neighbor

● This eternally grouchy resident of Bikini Bottom lives in a statue from Easter Island (known as a moai) in between SpongeBob and Patrick. The only time he seems to really be happy is when he plays the clarinet.

Squidward Tentacles • 2009

Bus Driver • 2008

Mrs. Puff • 2007

Doctor • 2008

Robot Customer • 2007

**Space suit**

### DID YOU KNOW?

SpongeBob SquarePants' creator has never revealed whether Squidward Tentacles is a squid or an octopus.

## Space Cadets

● SpongeBob and the gang donned space suits for their mission to net some alien jellyfish. To help them out, Sandy Cheeks built the intergalactic explorers a rocket and a moon buggy.

Sandy Cheeks Astronaut • 2008

SpongeBob SquarePants Astronaut • 2008

Patrick Astronaut • 2008

# LEGO® AVATAR™: THE LAST AIRBENDER™

Released in 2006 and based on the hugely popular animated Nickelodeon series, Avatar: The Last Airbender follows the adventures of Aang. His world is divided into four elements—Earth, Water, Fire, and Air—and he is the only person who can manipulate them all. Since each element has a distinct fighting style, Aang must master them all in order to maintain harmony.

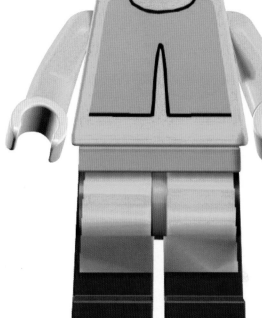

Master Airbender tattoo

### Aang

● The main protagonist, and last surviving Airbender, Aang is monk-in-training of the Air Nomads.

Aang • 2006

**DID YOU KNOW?**

When Aang was young, he revealed he was the Avatar when he chose four toys out of thousands, each of which were the childhood toys of the previous Avatars.

**DID YOU KNOW?**

The Chinese characters over the Avatar logo mean "the divine medium who has descended upon the mortal world."

Scar

Fireproof armor

Momo • 2006

Loops of hair

Katara Ninja • 2006

Sokka • 2006

### Prince Zuko

● Zuko is a banished Fire Nation prince and son of Fire Lord Ozai who is obsessed with capturing Aang to restore his lost honor.

Fire Nation Soldier • 2006

Mask

Firebender • 2006

Zuko • 2006

# LEGO® BATMAN™

This theme was introduced in 2006 and was based on characters from the DC Comics Universe, *Batman: The Animated Series*, and *The Dark Knight*. A young Bruce Wayne witnessed his parents being gunned down by a mugger. From that day forward, he vowed to use his wealth and power to fight crime and protect the innocent.

Alfred • 2006

### Bruce Wayne

● Batman's alter ego is billionaire playboy and philanthropist Bruce Wayne, who is the head of Wayne Enterprises and a respected Gotham City businessman.

Bruce Wayne • 2006

Utility belt

Batman • 2008

## Dynamic Duo

● Whether it's on land, in the air, or underwater, this crime-fighting twosome has just one goal: Rid Gotham City of evil forever. Batman™ prefers to use the Tumbler or the Batcyle to take down crooks like the Joker, while Robin chases outlaws like the Penguin in his Scuba Jet.

Robin 2006

Batman • 2006

Batman • 2007

Robin • 2008

## The Ice Man

● Mr. Freeze is one coldhearted villain. He plans all of his crimes around ice and snow, so if you feel a chilly breeze, you'd better watch out!

Cryogenic suit

Mr. Freeze™ • 2008

Catwoman™ • 2006

Killer Croc™ • 2006

## The Penguin

● A short, mobster-style criminal, Penguin is one of Batman's mortal enemies. He loves birds, and umbrellas and comes from a rich, high society family.

Poison Ivy™ • 2006

Nightwing™ • 2006

Penguin™ • 2006

Penguin™ • 2008

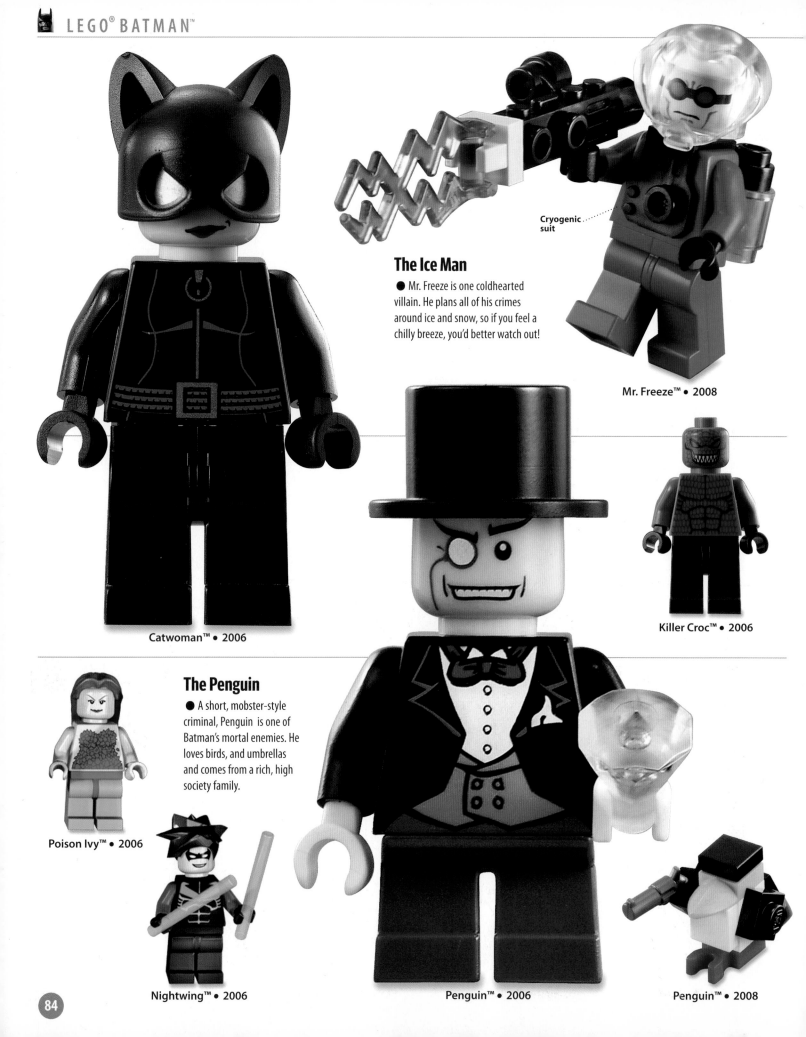

## The Joker

● The Joker was just a small-time crook until he fell into a vat of noxious toxins. The toxins dyed his skin white and his hair green and turned him into a madman. Now he terrorizes Gotham City with his henchmen. You always know when the Joker has committed a crime, because he will leave a joker playing card to mark his work.

**DID YOU KNOW?**

All the LEGO® Batman™ set-boxes feature comic strips by artist Greg Hyland, which depict stylised versions of the set.

Harley Quinn™ • 2008

Joker-gas ice cream

Henchman • 2008

## Two Face

● Two Face makes all decisions in his life by flipping a two-sided coin, one side of which has an "X" scratched on it.

The Joker™ • 2006

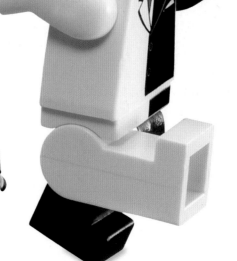

Bane™ • 2007

Scythe

Scarecrow™ • 2006

The Riddler™ • 2006

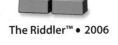

Two Face™ • 2006

# LEGO® INDIANA JONES™

Based on the *Indiana Jones™* movies, this theme was introduced in 2008. The swashbuckling archaeologist has discovered the Ark of the Covenant, drunk from the Holy Grail, and survived a nuclear blast inside a fridge. Two new Temple of Doom sets were released in 2009.

Indiana Jones™ • 2008

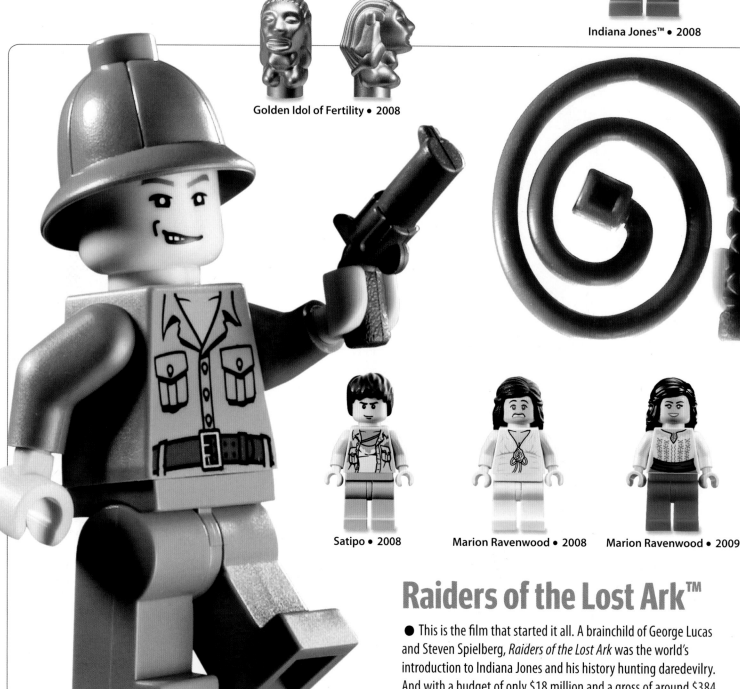

Golden Idol of Fertility • 2008

Satipo • 2008

Marion Ravenwood • 2008

Marion Ravenwood • 2009

René Belloq • 2008

## Raiders of the Lost Ark™

● This is the film that started it all. A brainchild of George Lucas and Steven Spielberg, *Raiders of the Lost Ark* was the world's introduction to Indiana Jones and his history hunting daredevilry. And with a budget of only $18 million and a gross of around $384 million, it is one of the most successful films of all time.

A LEGO® *Indiana Jones*™ videogame was released in 2008 that covers the first three movies.

**René Belloq • 2008**

**German Soldier 1 • 2008**

**German Soldier 2 • 2008**

**German Soldier 3 • 2008**

Pistol

**German Pilot • 2008**

**Swordsman • 2008**

Club

**Cairo Henchman • 2008**

**Indiana Jones™ • 2008**

# The Last Crusade

● Finally fans had a chance to meet Indy's dad in this film, played by the incomparable Sean Connery. Father and son reunite to track down the most prized of all archaeological treasures, the Holy Grail.

**Henry Jones Snr. • 2008**

**Indiana Jones • 2009**

**Elsa Schneider • 2009**

If you look closely at the hieroglyphics in the Lost Tomb set, you will find a miniature picture of R2-D2 and C-3PO from *Star Wars*™!

Fez

**Kazim • 2009**

**Willie Scott • 2009**

**Short Round • 2009**

**Indiana Jones™ • 2009**

# Temple of Doom

● After being chased out of Shanghai by gangsters, Indy, his sidekick Short Round, and his love interest Willie Scott flee to India. There they end up in pursuit of the sacred Sankara Stone, which pits them against the vicious Thuggee cult that believes in human sacrifice. Indy narrowly avoids becoming an offering to their dark gods before escaping their clutches and recovering the ancient treasure.

**Indiana Jones™ • 2009**

**Willie Scott • 2009**

**Gangster 1 • 2009**

**DID YOU KNOW?**

In the *LEGO Indiana Jones: The Original Adventures* video game, players can choose to be 83 different characters from the films or they can create a new one.

**Mola Ram • 2009**

**Gangster 2 • 2009**

Turban

**Chief Thuggee Guard • 2009**

**Thuggee Guard • 2009**

# The Kingdom of the Crystal Skull

● Indiana Jones and Mutt head off to Peru to find the mythical Crystal Skull of Akator, but will they find it before the evil Russians do? It's a high-spirited race to the prize as Indy and his cohorts dodge grave robbers, Ugha warriors, and Russian soldiers.

**Marion Ravenwood • 2008**

**Mutt • 2008**

Indiana Jones's accessories include a whip, a fedora, a leather pouch, and a pistol.

**Indiana Jones™ • 2008**

Binoculars

**Russian Guard 1 • 2008**

**Russian Guard 2 • 2008**

**Irina Spalko • 2008**

**Colonel Dovchenko • 2008**

## DID YOU KNOW?

Toys R Us released a limited edition set ("Peril in Peru") to commemorate the release of *The Kingdom of the Crystal Skull*™.

Crystal skull

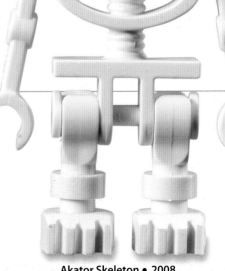

## DID YOU KNOW?

The Kingdom of the Crystal Skull set features a hidden room, skull launchers, shooting darts, and a spinning staircase.

**Ugha Warrior™ 1 • 2008**

**Ugha Warrior™ 2 • 2008**

**Grave Robber 1 • 2008**

**Grave Robber 2 • 2008**

**Skeleton • 2008**

**Akator Skeleton • 2008**

# LEGO® SPEED RACER™

Based on the special effects-filled 2008 film by the Wachowski Brothers (creators of *The Matrix* trilogy), this adrenalin-fueled theme follows Speed Racer as he goes up against the evil Royalton Industries. Will he be able to defeat them, win the Casa Cristo 5000, and figure out who the mysterious Racer X really is?

Speed Racer • 2008

### Girl Power

● Trixie's favorite color is pink. As Speed Racer's girlfriend she can sometimes be distracted by jealousy, but when she is piloting her helicopter during races to act as her boyfriend's spotter, she is all business.

Trixie • 2008

**White racing overalls**

Speed Racer • 2008

## The Need for Speed

● Speed Racer is an up-and-coming driver who plans on taking the racing world by storm. He has the need for speed in his blood because his parents build racecars for a living and his older brother, Rex, was a record-setting racer.

**DID YOU KNOW?**
Speed Racer was originally a Japanese animated TV series. It became a hit with US viewers when shown there in the 1960s.

Commentator • 2008

### Ruff Daddy
● Pops Racer is a former wrestler who you don't want to mess with, though he laughs as much as he fights. As the owner of Racer Motors, he is constantly inventing new supercharged engines, including Speed Racer's record-breaking racecars.

Pops Racer • 2008

Taejo Togokahn • 2008

Cruncher Block • 2008

Cruncher's Driver • 2008

X symbol

Taejo Togokhan • 2008

Racer X • 2008

### DID YOU KNOW?
Taejo Togokhan's racecar has the name Togokhan Motors printed on it in the Korean alphabet of Hangul.

Cannonball Taylor • 2008

Snake Oiler • 2008

91

# FAN FIGURES

As soon as minifigures made their debut in 1978, fans started customizing them. They created completely new characters using official LEGO® parts and then adding their own stickers, paint jobs, and handmade accessories. Suddenly a banker's torso with a formal black jacket might be used to make an Abraham Lincoln minifigure.

No one knew just how popular these customized minifigures would become, but over the years MOCs (My Own Creations) have become a vital part of the LEGO fan experience. Go online these days and you will see thousands of these one-of-a-kind minifigures. You might recognize some characters from movies, comic books, or television shows, but others are purely the work of the creator's imagination.

Aegis • 2008

Conquistador de la Muerta • 2008

Chinese guy • 2008

Senneri • 2008

Morgan • 2008

Red Samurai • 2008

Abraham Lincoln • 2008

Ice Breaker • 2008

US Marine in Dress Uniform • 2008

Kobaziku • 2008

John Booker • 2008

Mark Twain • 2008

**DID YOU KNOW?**

If you type "customized LEGO minifigure" into Google, you get almost 40,000 images ranging from a light-up Iron Man to President Barack Obama.

Benjamin Franklin • 2008

Oberstik • 2008

Nakko Chan • 2008

Nevin Martell • 2009

Black Samurai • 2008

A whole community has sprung up and these pages highlight some of the phenomenal work out there. From famous historical figures to futuristic steampunk warriors, many talented customizers have truly allowed their imagination to run wild. If these minifigures get your own creative juices going, start thinking about what custom minifigures you would like to make.

# LEGO® DIGITAL

In 1997, the first LEGO® computer game was released—LEGO Island, followed by LEGO Loco and LEGO Chess the following year. Since then many more themes have moved into the gaming world giving LEGO fans even more scope for creativity. Coming up next in the LEGO digital world is LEGO Universe, an interactive massively multiplayer game which will allow players to customize their own characters and weapons in a vitrual LEGO world.

1998          1998

LEGO Creator game • 1998

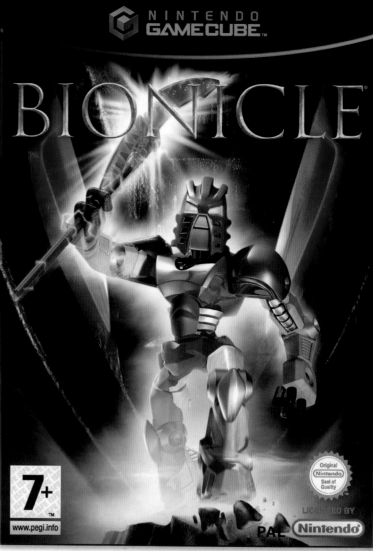

BIONICLE® game • 2003

1999       2001       2000       2000       2000

## DID YOU KNOW?

LEGO® *Star Wars*™: The Video Game has sold around 5.92 million copies, combining the sales of all platforms.

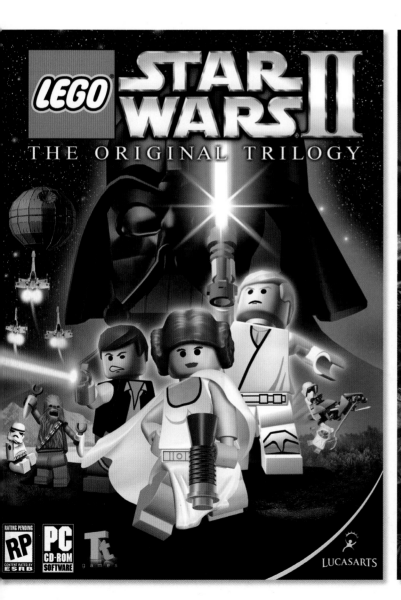

LEGO® *Star Wars*™ II game • 2006

LEGO® *Indiana Jones*™ game • 2008

LONDON, NEW YORK,
MELBOURNE, MUNICH, AND DELHI

## For DK
**Editor** Vicki Taylor
**Designer** Anne Sharples
**Managing Editor** Catherine Saunders
**Art Director** Lisa Lanzarini
**Publishing Manager** Simon Beecroft
**Category Publisher** Alex Allan
**Production Editor** Clare McLean
**Production Controller** Nick Seston

## For the LEGO Group
Randi Kirsten Sørensen, Keith Malone, Stephanie Lawrence, Matthew James Ashton,
Chriss Bonven Johansen and the Graphic Lab team, Jette Orduna, Edel Schwarz Andersen and Mona B. Petersen

First published in the United States in 2009 by
DK Publishing,
375 Hudson Street, New York, New York 10014

ISBN: 978-0-75665-623-2

LD114 07/09

Colour reproduction by Alta Image, UK
Printed and bound in China by Hung Hing

ACKNOWLEDGMENTS
DK would like to thank: Heather Scott, Laura Gilbert, Lucy Dowling, and Julia March for editorial assistance, Lisa Sodeau for design assistance, and Lisa Lanzarini for the jacket design.

Discover more at
www.dk.com
www.LEGO.com